SMART STRUCTURES

BRIDGES

Julie Richards

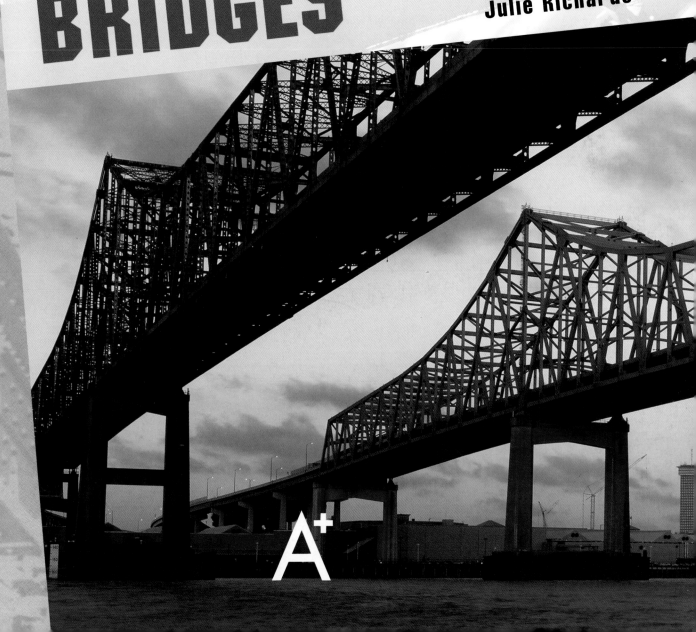

A+

This edition first published in 2004 in the United States of America by Smart Apple Media.

Smart Apple Media
1980 Lookout Drive
North Mankato
Minnesota 56003

Library of Congress Cataloging-in-Publication Data

Richards, Julie.
  Bridges / by Julie Richards.
    p. cm. — (Smart structures)
  Summary: Describes four kinds of bridges, the methods and materials of their construction, and amazing or disastrous examples.
  ISBN 1-58340-344-2
  1. Bridges—Design and construction—Juvenile literature. [1. Bridges—Design and construction.] I. Title.
  TG148.R513 2003
  624'.2—dc21   2002044632

First Edition
9 8 7 6 5 4 3 2 1

First published in 2003 by
MACMILLAN EDUCATION AUSTRALIA PTY LTD
627 Chapel Street, South Yarra, Australia 3141

Associated companies and representatives throughout the world.

Edited by Anna Fern
Text design by Cristina Neri, Canary Graphic Design
Cover design by Cristina Neri, Canary Graphic Design
Layout by Nina Sanadze
Illustrations by Margaret Hastie, IKON Computergraphics
Photo research by Legend Images

Printed in Thailand

Acknowledgements
The author and the publisher are grateful to the following for permission to reproduce copyright material:

Cover photograph: Greater New Orleans Bridge, U.S., courtesy of Getty Images.

Australian Picture Library/Corbis, pp. 5 (bottom right), 13; Coo-ee Picture Library, p. 24; Corbis Digital Stock, p. 7 (bottom); Digital Vision, p. 11; Getty Images, pp. 1, 4, 5 (top left), 7 (top), 9, 10, 19, 20, 23, 27, 28 (top), 29; Honshu-Shikoku Bridge Authority (HSBA), pp. 5 (bottom left), 21; Copyright K'NEX Industries, Inc. used with permission, p. 30; Legend Images, p. 15; Brian Parker, pp. 5 (top right), 17; Photolibrary.com, pp. 16, 28 (bottom); Reuters, pp. 14, 25, 26.

While every care has been taken to trace and acknowledge copyright, the publisher tenders their apologies for any accidental infringement where copyright has proved untraceable. Where the attempt has been unsuccessful, the publisher welcomes information that would redress the situation.

CONTENTS

KEY WORDS

When a word is printed in **bold** you can look up its meaning in the key words box on the same page. You can also look up the meaning of words in the glossary on page 31.

BRIDGES AS STRUCTURES

A **structure** is made up of many different parts joined together. The shapes of the parts and the way they are joined together help a structure to stand up and do the job for which it has been designed. The **materials** used to make a structure can be made stronger or weaker, depending on their shape and how they are put together.

Bridges are made by humans, but there are also natural bridges. For as long as people have wanted to move from one place to another, they have built bridges. Bridges are built to:

- make journeys for land vehicles and pedestrians shorter, safer, and easier
- carry goods from one place to another as quickly and cheaply as possible
- make journeys across water easier and more comfortable than taking a ferry
- quickly carry traffic away from cities, easing traffic jams and pollution
- cross land that is too rough or not solid enough to support a road.

This natural bridge was made by wind and water rubbing away the rock over many thousands of years.

KEY WORDS

structure something that is made up of many parts joined together

materials anything used to make a structure

Types of bridges

There are four types of bridges made by humans:

- **beam** bridges
- arch bridges
- **suspension** bridges
- cable-stayed bridges.

The type of bridge that is built depends on what it is needed for and the place where it is to be built.

This stone arch bridge, built by the ancient Romans more than 2,000 years ago, carried water into towns and cities.

This beam bridge, in Austria, carries traffic across a valley. It makes the journey much shorter for travelers.

Cable-stayed bridges have wide gaps between their supports to allow large ships through.

This suspension bridge in Japan joins many small islands together so people can drive rather than travel by ferry.

If you look very closely at a bridge, you will notice:

- the different parts which have been joined together to build the bridge
- the shapes of these parts.

Bridges must carry extremely heavy loads. Wind, earthquakes, and moving traffic make a bridge bend and shake. It is important that the parts of a bridge are made in the right shapes and joined together the right way, or the bridge will not be safe.

Bridge shapes

Some shapes are stronger than others. Rectangles, arches, and triangles are the strongest shapes used to build big structures, but they all have their breaking point.

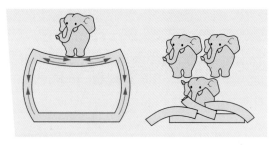

Rectangle

One elephant on a rectangle makes the top side bend. The weight of three elephants causes the top side to break.

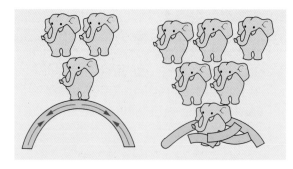

Arch

The weight of three elephants on an arch spreads along the curve to the ground below. The weight of six elephants causes the sides to spread apart and collapse.

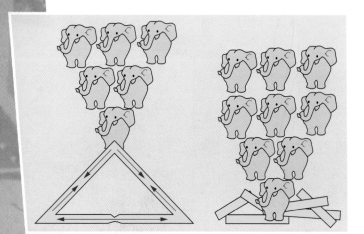

Triangle

The weight of six elephants on a triangle causes the two top sides to squeeze together and the bottom side to pull apart. The triangle is the strongest shape, but a herd of elephants makes the bottom side stretch so much that it snaps in half.

Can weaker shapes be made stronger?

Rectangles are not as strong as triangles. Rectangles can be made stronger by using extra pieces of building material to make them into triangles. An extra piece like this is called a **brace**.

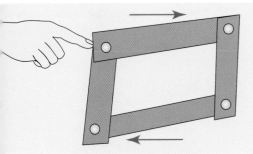 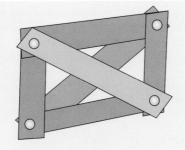 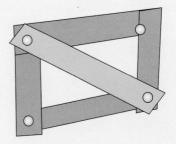

The sides of a rectangle are weak and can be easily moved about.

Fixing two pieces of material to a rectangle makes it stiffer and stronger.

One of the extra pieces can be taken away without weakening the rectangle.

When a giraffe bends over to drink, its long neck makes it very unstable. So the giraffe spreads its front legs to make a strong, stable triangle. ▶

Triangles

Triangles are the strongest, stiffest, and most **stable** of all the shapes. Triangles are used to make many different everyday things. You can go on a great triangle hunt! See how many things you can find that use triangles in their structure. Here are a few clues:

- shelves can be held up by triangles
- bicycles and kites are made up of triangles
- some types of chairs use triangles to make them stable
- some triangles reach high into the sky—they hold up electricity wires or lift heavy objects on building sites.

Perhaps you can see where some rectangles have been braced and made into triangles.

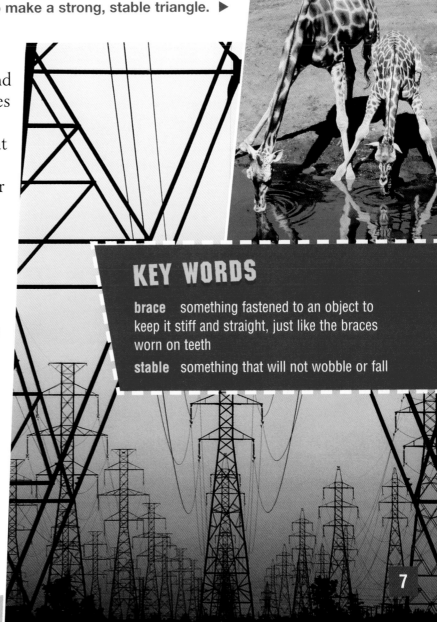

KEY WORDS

brace something fastened to an object to keep it stiff and straight, just like the braces worn on teeth

stable something that will not wobble or fall

These electricity towers are braced with triangles. ▶

THE PARTS OF A BRIDGE

All bridges have foundations, piers, and decks. Without these, a bridge cannot do the job for which it has been designed.

Foundations

The foundations of a bridge are a firm base upon which the bridge is built. Like the roots of a tree, they go deep into the ground and stop the bridge from toppling over in the wind or sinking under its own weight. Most bridge foundations are holes filled with concrete and super-strong metal. Bridges bounce or shake a little when heavy traffic rumbles across them. The foundations soak up the shaking just like a sponge and send it into the ground around them.

Piers and decks

Piers are huge towers built on top of the foundations. The towers on the Humber Bridge, in England, are two inches (4 cm) farther apart at the top than the bottom. Why? To allow for the curving surface of Earth! The piers are wider at the bottom to prevent the bridge from being seriously damaged should a ship or heavy vehicle crash into one of them.

The piers hold up the top part of the bridge, called the deck. The deck is where the road, railroad, or sidewalk is laid to carry the load the bridge has been designed for.

▼ All bridges have foundations, piers, and decks.

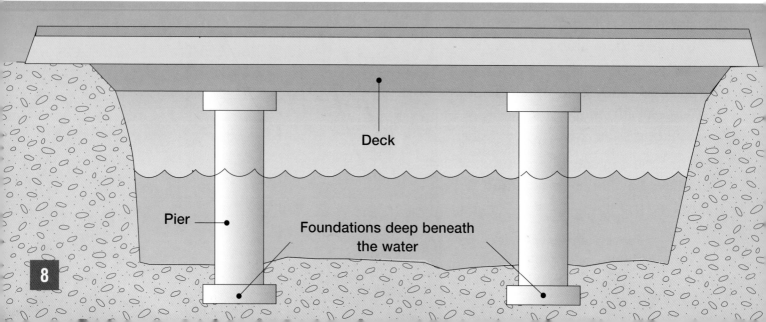

Deck

Pier

Foundations deep beneath the water

Allowing for movement

The parts used in bridge building must be **flexible**. Some bridges can sway 6 to 10 feet (2–3 m) in strong winds. **Engineers** design bridges so that they can move with the wind, just as a tree does. If a tree did not sway, its trunk would snap.

As heavy traffic rolls across a bridge, the bridge sags slightly. Strong pieces of metal, called bearing plates, sit between beams and piers and allow the beams to slide and twist a little.

Changes in the weather can make parts of a bridge swell or shrink. Bridges have joints made from a special spongy material that can spring back into shape after being stretched or squeezed. These joints are called **expansion** joints. This allows the bridge to move slightly without breaking.

Four-legged animals are like bridges. The four legs act like piers. The weight hangs from the backbone, but is supported by muscles and tendons which move like cables. Engineers get many of their ideas from nature.

KEY WORDS

flexible able to bend without breaking

engineers people who design and build large structures

expansion growing or getting bigger

BUILDING MATERIALS

The first bridge builders used the natural materials they found around them. An early bridge was usually a fallen tree or piles of flat stones placed across a narrow stream. The first small suspension bridges were made from thick, tough plant vines knotted together and tied to strong trees. The first modern bridges were made of iron. Today, most bridges are made of steel and concrete.

This suspension bridge, in Papua New Guinea, is made from vines and wood. ▶

Steel

Steel is made mostly of iron and is used to make the parts of a bridge that need to be super strong. Steel is lighter than iron and can stretch. In beam and arch bridges, steel is used to make arches, **girders**, and **trusses**. In suspension and cable-stayed bridges, it is used for towers and suspension cables. A steel cable as thick as your finger could lift a 33-ton (30-t) truck!

◀ These bridges use lots of triangles in the trusses that make up their structure.

Concrete

Concrete is a mixture of **cement**, water, sand, and gravel. The wet, runny mixture is poured into molds so that it can be shaped into girders and beams or into blocks to build piers and towers. Concrete dries to become strong and hard as rock. A mug-sized piece of concrete could support a 33-ton (30-t) truck! Concrete cracks quite easily when it is stretched. Pouring wet concrete over bunches of steel wires, or a grid of steel bars, strengthens the concrete and stops it from cracking as it stretches. This is called **reinforced** concrete. Reinforced concrete is used in the foundations and beams of many large structures.

Future materials

Engineers are busy developing lighter, stronger materials from which bridges can be built. Materials such as **Kevlar** are stronger and lighter than steel, but very expensive to use in large bridges.

In the United States, there is a bridge made mostly from recycled waste plastic. Reusing waste plastic helps the environment by solving the very large problem of what to do with waste that does not break down. The plastic parts of the bridge are not as expensive to look after as steel or wooden parts.

The road deck on the proposed Gibraltar Straits Bridge, between Spain and north Africa, will be made from **fiberglass**. Fiberglass can last for 100 years, is easily repaired, and can be laid in a few days. Concrete would take three months to pour.

Can you see the steel wires sticking out from the reinforced concrete piers on this unfinished bridge?

KEY WORDS

cement an ingredient in concrete which makes the concrete harden like stone

reinforced made stronger

Kevlar very strong human-made material

fiberglass a material made with threads of glass

BRIDGE DESIGN

Engineers do a lot of research to make sure the right type of bridge is designed for the job it has to do. Science has helped engineers find out about stronger bridge designs, lighter building materials, and new tools that do the job faster. Bridge engineers use many of the shapes that are seen in nature. Shapes such as arches and triangles have proved to be extremely strong and stable for bridge building.

Beam bridges

A beam bridge is the simplest type of bridge. A short beam bridge is a single beam with supports at each end. Beam bridges like this can only span a small gap. Without supports beneath the middle part of the bridge, the beams will collapse under their own weight.

Wherever possible, engineers choose beam bridges with short beams and lots of piers to support them underneath, because they are cheaper and easier to build. The beams can be made of concrete or steel and shaped into girders and trusses.

Beam bridges are used to carry railroad or road traffic. The Forth Railway Bridge, in Scotland, is a type of beam bridge called a cantilever bridge. It has a series of beams that span the Forth River like outstretched arms.

The first railroads used iron-beam bridges to carry trains over rocky or swampy land, across deep valleys, and around hills. This meant that the heavy steam trains did not have to slow down and could reach their destination faster.

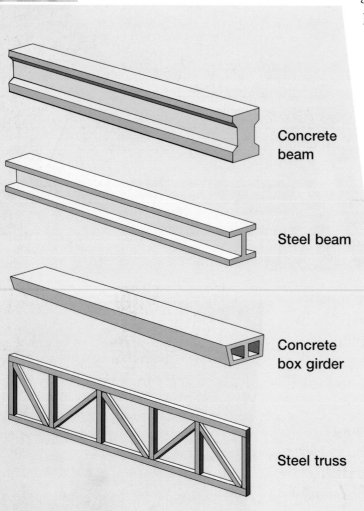

Concrete beam

Steel beam

Concrete box girder

Steel truss

◀ Here are four different kinds of beams.

Arch bridges

Arch bridges are used to carry traffic, railroads, pedestrians, and **canals** over roads, rivers, and steep valleys. Some bridges are thousands of years old. The ancient Romans found that wooden beam bridges could only take a small amount of weight and soon rotted because they were not protected from the weather. Arch bridges built from small stones or bricks were weatherproof and much stronger. The Romans invented a type of cement and found that by joining many arches together, they could span a large gap.

Spandrels

▲ Iron Bridge at Coalbrookdale, England, was built in 1779.

Older arch bridges are usually made of solid stone or brick. The first iron-arch bridge ever built was the Iron Bridge across the Severn River at Coalbrookdale, in England. Arch bridges like this have connections called **spandrels**.

Modern arch bridges are built of steel trusses and concrete. Some of the massive steel truss arches are more than 1,641 feet (500 m) long and as high as a 60-story building! The decks on most modern arch bridges are supported by the arch underneath. The Sydney Harbor Bridge, in Australia, is different—its deck is hung below the giant arch on steel spandrels.

Suspension bridges

Suspension bridges are the giants of the bridge world. They can span half a mile (1 km) or more. Their decks hang from thick steel cables draped over enormous concrete and steel towers which are **anchored** to the ground at each end of the bridge. Suspension bridges are ideal for carrying traffic across wide stretches of water.

A suspension bridge does not need lots of piers to support its beams from underneath. This means that large and tall-masted ships can easily pass beneath a suspension bridge without scraping the underside of the bridge's deck or being dragged by fast-flowing water into the piers. Smaller suspension bridges are often used as footbridges across the space between steep cliffs.

The Golden Gate Bridge, in the U.S., is the most famous suspension bridge in the world. Can you see the triangles in its structure?

Before long suspension bridges were built, people would have to take a slow ferryboat across the water or travel a long way up a river before they could find a place narrow enough to support a beam bridge.

The Akashi Kaikyo suspension bridge, which links the small islands of Japan, is the longest suspension bridge in the world. Its longest span is 6,531 feet (1,990 m), or more than a mile (2 km) without a support! It takes 20 minutes to walk from tower to tower on one span.

Cable-stayed bridges

A cable-stayed bridge is like a suspension bridge because strong, steel cables support its deck. The cables that support the deck of a suspension bridge are draped over the towers at each end and fixed in the ground. A cable-stayed bridge is different. Its cables are attached to the towers themselves and fan out along the deck. This makes a cable-stayed bridge easier and cheaper to build, because it uses fewer materials. However, without deep ground anchors, a cable-stayed bridge cannot have spans as long as a suspension bridge. The tower of a suspension or cable-stayed bridge can be as high as a skyscraper. The deck is shaped so that the air flows around it. Otherwise the deck would vibrate like a plucked guitar string when it was windy.

A cable-stayed bridge in Sydney, Australia ▼

Choosing the right bridge design

Choosing a bridge design depends on different things. Engineers decide what sort of foundations are needed and how deep they should be after geologists test samples of rock and soil in a laboratory to discover if there are any weaknesses in the ground. Next, the engineers will work out how much the bridge will weigh and how much extra weight it will carry when it is in use. This tells the engineers how strong the bridge parts need to be. They must try and keep the bridge as light as possible without making it weak.

BUILDING BRIDGES

Building a large bridge is an enormous job which can take hundreds of people more than five years to finish.

Foundations and piers

Digging the foundations and building the **embankments** are the first jobs to be done on any bridge. Each embankment slopes gently up to the bridge so that the road is raised to the same level as the road deck. Powerful earth-moving machines do most of this work. If the ground is soft, the foundations will be dug by huge spinning **pile drivers** until harder rock is felt. If the soft ground goes very deep, concrete slabs will be poured into molds. The slabs act like rafts and will spread the vibration and weight over a larger distance. If you toss a pebble into water, the farther the ripples spread, the less power they have. A concrete slab foundation does a similar thing.

KEY WORDS

embankments mounds of earth made by humans to carry a road or railroad

pile drivers powerful machines that push large metal or concrete poles into the ground like a hammer

abutments supports at the end of a bridge

As the piers and **abutments** are built on top of the foundations, another mold is made for the concrete to be poured into. The mold is made from wooden sheets or steel plates, called formwork, and is supported by a special frame called scaffolding. Huge cranes are used to lower bunches of steel wires into each mold to reinforce the concrete. Wet concrete is poured into the mold and allowed to set. The formwork is then moved up and more concrete is poured and allowed to set. This goes on until the pier reaches the right height.

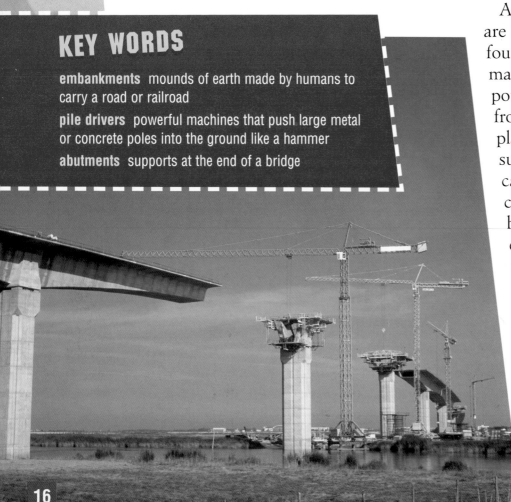

◀ Long piers are built in stages.

Building a beam bridge

The beams for a beam bridge may be made of steel or concrete. If it is a long bridge, the beams are usually made in a factory and brought to the bridge site, where they are lifted into place by a crane. For spans only a few feet long, concrete beams can be poured on the spot, using formwork as a mold. The beams are laid side by side. Bearing plates are placed in between the beams and the piers and abutments. Formwork is built along the sides so that concrete can be poured for the road deck. Finally, expansion joints are placed at the end of the beams.

A beam bridge carries the weight straight down into the ground through its piers and abutments. Special joints and plates allow the bridge to move, adjusting to temperature, wind and Earth movements, and the vibration from traffic rolling across the beams.

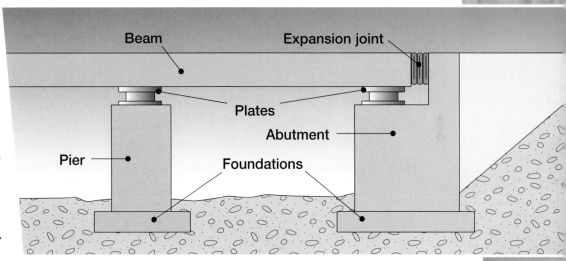

Cantilever bridges

A cantilever is a beam fixed at just one end. A diving board is similar to a cantilever beam. What happens as you walk further down a diving board? It sags under your weight.

A large cantilever bridge needs extra pillars to support its central beams. Each section of a cantilever bridge has a central pillar with a beam sticking out from either side. It looks like a letter "T" or a pair of outstretched arms. A high, arching middle span joins the pillars and allows ships to pass beneath.

The Forth Railway Bridge, in Scotland, is the most famous cantilever bridge in the world. Finished in 1890, it was the first bridge to be made mostly of steel—65,000 tons (59,000 t) of it. Almost seven million **rivets** were needed to fasten the steel tubing and girders together.

The Forth Railway Bridge, in Scotland ▶

Building an arch bridge

Arch bridges have great natural strength. Most of the bridges you see in nature are still standing because they are arch shaped. The weight of an arch bridge is evenly spread around the arch to its ends, which are firmly anchored in the ground.

Older stone-arch bridges were usually built between two thick brick or stone piers around a temporary frame. The last stone to be added was the wedge-shaped keystone. The keystone was always placed at the top of the arch. With the keystone in position, all the blocks beneath pushed on each other and no cement was needed. The frame was removed after the arch was finished.

These early arches were high and narrow, and several would be needed to cross a wide river. Strong abutments and piers were needed to prevent the sides of the arch from "doing the splits." Some of the piers were so wide that they blocked most of the river and the water wore away the stonework.

The Trajans Bridge was built across the Danube River, in Europe, by the ancient Romans around A.D. 104. It had 21 arches stretching more than 3,000 feet (914 m) and contained more than a million stones. Each stone weighed about half a ton (450 kg). The Romans used cranes driven by giant wheels to lift the stones into place. Men ran inside the wheels, making them turn, allowing the cranes to work. As the arches reached higher, the builders climbed scaffolding made from wooden poles tied together to reach the top of the bridge. The bridge was destroyed by the Romans 150 years later, as they retreated in battle.

Arch bridges can be filled with stone or brick, or have metal connections, called spandrels.

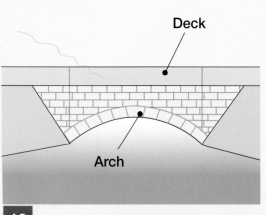

Filled arch

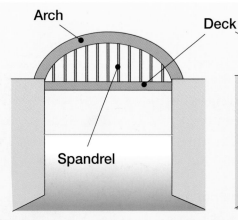

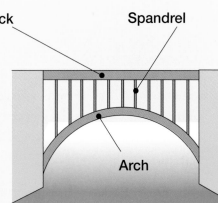

Spandrel arches

Modern arch bridges

With the development of modern building materials such as steel and concrete, engineers found that they could build bigger arches. This meant that they could build an arch bridge over a deep, wide expanse of water without large piers getting in the way of shipping. The Sydney Harbor Bridge in Sydney, Australia, is the world's largest and widest modern steel arch bridge. It spans 1,650 feet (503 m) and carries four railroad lines, eight road-traffic lanes, a sidewalk, and a bicycle path. Most arch bridges have the deck above the arch. The Sydney Harbor Bridge has its deck hung below. The arch may rise or fall seven inches (18 cm) as the steel swells or shrinks during warm or cool weather.

▲ Sydney Harbor Bridge
was opened in 1932.

Sydney Harbor Bridge was built without a framework, so that ships could still use the harbor. Two steel arches were built out from each bank and were held up by 128 cables anchored underground through U-shaped tunnels. The 250 workers and their families lived in a camp nearby. Three ships were specially built to carry the enormous numbered blocks of rock used in the towers 186 miles (300 km) from where they were cut. Steel girders were made in workshops, placed onto barges, towed into position, and lifted up by two 640-ton (580-t) electrically operated cranes, which built the arches before them as they moved slowly forward. Up to 96 steam railroad engines were driven onto the bridge to test its strength.

Building a suspension bridge

A suspension bridge is a bit like a tent. A tent only stays up if its ropes are stretched equally and attached to pegs pushed deep into firm ground. The stretched ropes pull on the tent from all sides, stopping the tent from collapsing.

The first suspension bridges had cables made of grass or vines. People soon discovered that by plaiting bunches of vines or grass together, they could make a rope strong enough to support the weight of people.

In the Himalaya Mountains, ancient bamboo and woven rattan suspension bridges had a hut at each end filled with stone to help anchor the bridge. The rope cables were wound around tree trunks beneath the huts. Wooden levers or handles extended from the tree trunks. People would hold these and turn the trunk. As the tree trunks were turned, the cables were pulled tighter, keeping the bridge stable. Some of these bridges are more than 229 feet (70 m) long and have been in use for more than 300 years.

Many of these older suspension bridges were quite short. They often swayed so much in windy weather, or under the weight and movement of the people using them, that the people crossing could become seasick.

The Menai Strait Bridge, in Wales, was the first successful long suspension bridge. This bridge was built by Thomas Telford in 1826. Its 581-foot-long (177-m) deck was hung on chains made from iron bars about 10 feet (3 m) long which were bolted together.

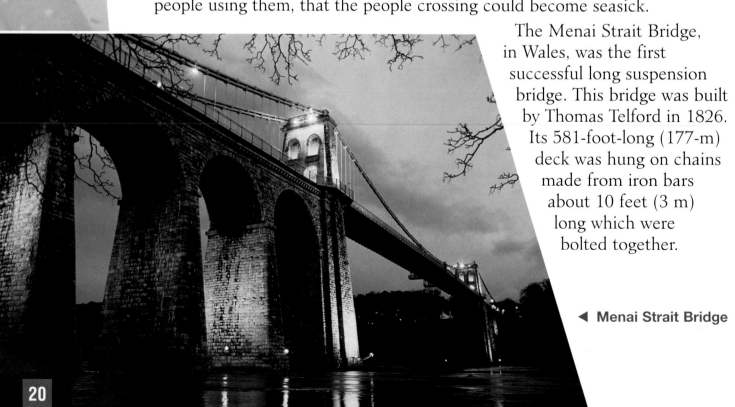

◄ Menai Strait Bridge

Modern suspension bridges

Modern suspension bridges have concrete towers resting on deep foundations. Steel cables are run across the tops of the towers and fixed into concrete anchors. The anchors have to be very heavy to stop the cables from being pulled out when the bridge deck sags as it carries traffic. One of the anchors for the Humber Bridge, in England, weighs 331,200 tons (300,000 t).

Huge concrete anchors hold the thick, steel cables of the Verrazano Narrows suspension bridge, in the U.S.

Suspension cables

Suspension cables are made by spinning thousands of thin steel wires together. A machine like a bicycle wheel runs up and down, picking up the strands and twisting them tightly together. Some cables are more than three feet (1 m) thick. The spun cables are placed inside steel tubes to protect them from the weather.

The Akashi Kaikyo Bridge, in Japan, is so long that its cables could circle Earth more than seven times! A groove in the tower stops the cable from slipping off. **Hangers** join the deck to the cables. The builders hang wire walkways between the towers so that they can hang the cables and fix the hangers. The deck is added one piece at a time. It is attached to cables, lifted on a hoist, and pulled along rails and into position. Once all the deck pieces are in place, some of the builders climb inside the hollow pieces and join them together by **welding**.

Building a cable-stayed bridge

A cable-stayed bridge is a newer type of suspension bridge which has been built since the 1950s. The difference between a cable-stayed bridge and a suspension bridge is how the deck pieces are joined and where the cables are placed.

In a cable-stayed bridge, the cables are anchored, or stayed, to the towers and fan out along the deck. The deck pieces are concrete. They are raised into position and pulled together on tight steel cables. The stretched cables pull and the vibration and weight of the traffic travels through them to the towers and down into the ground.

If you have ever been in a tug-of-war where the other team is as strong as your team, you can see how the pulling action of a cable-stayed or suspension bridge works. The steel cables are like spider-web silk—light, but tough, and spun in tight spirals for extra strength. Just as a spider's web is anchored firmly to another structure, so the cables are anchored to the bridge towers.

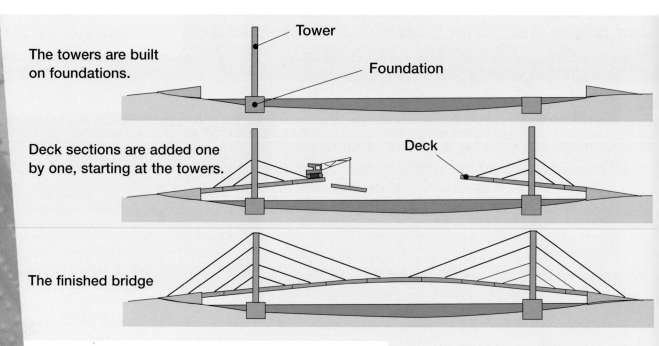

The towers are built on foundations.

Tower

Foundation

Deck sections are added one by one, starting at the towers.

Deck

The finished bridge

▲ This is how a cable-stayed bridge is built.

Sometimes, there are two different types of ground where the foundations of a bridge are to be built. The Tamar River in Tasmania, Australia, has hard rock on one side and soft clay on the other. So, a half-suspension, half-cable-stayed bridge was designed, which supports nearly all the weight of the Batman Bridge from the rocky side.

Building across water

Suspension and cable-stayed bridges are usually built across wide rivers or bays, with their towers standing in water.

Staying dry

Keeping the work area dry and free of mud while foundations are dug and towers are built can be a problem. If the water is shallow, a temporary circular dam called a cofferdam is built in the river. The water is pumped out and the soft river mud is dug away until harder ground is felt. The bottom is lined with concrete.

One of the piers for the Golden Gate Bridge, in the U.S., had to be built in the open ocean, 1,000 feet (305 m) below the surface. The engineer built a cofferdam that was large enough to enclose a playing field. Hundreds of tons of concrete were pumped in.

In deeper water, a concrete tube called a caisson is used. The mud is dug out from inside and the caisson sinks until it reaches solid rock. Concrete is pumped in and the caisson becomes the foundation for the tower.

The Brooklyn Bridge, in New York, was the first bridge where explosives were used inside a caisson to break up rock.

Decks and cables

When a bridge is built across a river, the deck pieces are floated on barges until they are in position beneath the bridge. Floating cranes lift deck pieces and equipment up to the deck height. The cranes pull a special rope into place so that a walkway can be built for the workers who will attach the cables. The water around the Akashi Kaikyo Bridge is crowded with shipping and flows so fast that a helicopter was used to pull the rope into position.

WORKING BRIDGES

Once a bridge is finished, it is prepared for use. The road surface is laid and safety fences are added. As well as lighting for the traffic using the bridge, lights are placed on the top of the bridge to show aircraft pilots where it is. Other lights are placed on the piers to alert shipping crews to the width between the piers and the height of the deck. Warning lights and speed signs are set up to tell drivers to slow down or avoid crossing when dangerously high winds are blowing. The bridge may not blow over, but gusts of wind can flip small or high-sided vehicles over.

▼ Warning signs and wind socks let drivers know that it is windy on this bridge.

Akashi Kaikyo Bridge

The Akashi Kaikyo Bridge, in Japan, is built in an area that is shaken by earthquakes, pounded by giant waves, and blasted by powerful winds. To cope with some of the worst weather on Earth, the engineers used frames of open triangles beneath the road deck that allow the wind to blow through the structure. Twenty special concrete blocks called tuned mass dampers (T.M.D.s) were placed in each tower. When high winds or an earthquake move the bridge in one direction, the T.M.D.s are moved in the opposite direction to balance the bridge and stop it from swaying. This design means the bridge can handle 180-mile-per-hour (289 km per hour) winds and very big earthquakes!

Looking after bridges

Bridges need to be checked regularly and looked after to make sure they stay safe and keep working properly. The people who work on bridges wear hard hats to protect their heads and safety harnesses that stop them from falling. Special trolleys, which slide up and down the steel tubes of suspension and cable-stayed bridges like mini roller-coasters, allow workers to check parts of the bridge that would be impossible to reach any other way. Bridges can be X-rayed to check for rust and cracking in parts that cannot be seen from outside. Cracking can let water reach the steel inside. Bridges also need to be painted regularly.

Painting

Bridges are often out in the rain or sitting in thick fog. Although steel and concrete are very strong, moisture and pollution can eat away at them, weakening the bridge structure. Layers of paint help protect against rusting. The steel deck on the Humber Bridge, in England, began to rust from the inside 11 years after the bridge was opened. Engineers used a chemical that soaks up moisture and a **device** like a giant hair dryer to stop it.

Workers sometimes ride on a special trolley to check parts that cannot be reached any other way.

KEY WORDS

device a machine or tool designed to do a particular job

25

BRIDGES THAT WENT WRONG

Most modern bridges are built to withstand earthquakes, high winds, floods, and heavy traffic. Sometimes, unexpected events such as a really big earthquake or a sudden flood can destroy them. In the past, some bridges went wrong because engineers did not understand how to make structures strong and stable by using the right shapes and materials. There were no computers or special tests that could tell them if the ground was solid enough to support a structure or if there were weaknesses in the bridge design.

The piers in this freeway did not have enough reinforcing steel to stop the bridge from collapsing during the 1995 earthquake in Kobe, Japan.

Tay Bridge

The Tay Bridge, in Scotland, was an early iron bridge that carried trains across a wide river from 1878 until 1879. There had been many problems building the foundations in the soft, slippery mud of the river-bed, and the iron was rusting badly. The girders groaned and shook whenever a train rolled over the bridge. One windy night, the iron girders twisted and tore apart just as a train went onto the bridge. Thirteen spans tumbled into the river below and 75 people were killed. The bridge that was built to replace it still stands today.

Tacoma Narrows Bridge

The Tacoma Narrows Bridge, in the U.S., collapsed in 1940 after it had only been open four months. Luckily, no one was killed when the bridge began to shake and ripple like an ocean wave as it tore to pieces in the wind. This showed engineers that suspension-bridge decks needed to be designed to stop them from shuddering violently in the wind.

Millennium Footbridge

The Millennium Footbridge across the river Thames in London, England, was closed only three days after it opened, in June 2000. The bridge swayed so much that when people walked on it they became seasick. Ninety shock absorbers were fitted to soak up the vibration of moving feet. Two thousand volunteers walked across the bridge to test it before it was reopened in February 2002.

The collapse of the Tacoma Narrows Bridge showed engineers that suspension-bridge decks needed to be built differently to cope with wind.

Sunshine Skyway Bridge

During a violent thunderstorm, in 1980, a ship crashed into the Sunshine Skyway Bridge in Florida, sending more than 1,000 feet (304 m) of the bridge into the Tampa Bay. A cable-stayed bridge was built to replace the steel cantilever.

Protecting the new bridge from ships was important. Large concrete islands, called dolphins, were placed around the bridge's six piers. The dolphins were designed to withstand the force of a 97,000-ton (88,392-t) ship hitting them. The steel tubes that hold the steel cables were painted bright yellow. The new bridge soars 190 feet (57 m) into the air to make it safer for ships to find their way through.

AMAZING BRIDGES

Some unusual bridges work in very clever and interesting ways. They are built when it is too expensive or not possible to build a high bridge.

Moving bridges

▼ Tower Bridge

Tower Bridge is a very famous bridge in London, England. The road deck of Tower Bridge is two separate pieces, each hinged at one end so that they can move. They can be lifted up like a drawbridge to let tall-masted ships through. Even though each piece weighs about 1,231 tons (1,117 t), the powerful motors inside the towers can lift them in four minutes.

A lift bridge can also be raised, but it works more like an elevator. The span of a lift bridge is attached to the towers at each end. As a ship approaches, motor-driven cables in each of the towers lift the span.

A swing bridge does not move up and down, but turns from side to side. The span is balanced at the center on a pier. There are wheels on the pier that swing the deck around to let ships pass and then swing it back to join up with the road on either side of the river.

If a river-bed is too soft to support a bridge, a floating pontoon bridge can be used. A pontoon bridge is a beam that can be made from hollow concrete blocks anchored to the river-bed by cables with a road or railroad placed on top. A pontoon bridge can also be a beam that floats on the water and carries people, just like a ferry.

This is a transporter bridge. Cars drive into a cage hanging from cables attached to the girders above. The cage is pulled across the river like a cable car or ski lift.

Bridge facts and firsts

Many of the world's most amazing structures are bridges. Some bridges are record-breakers because of their size or their design. Other bridges are famous because they were the first to use certain building materials or because ways of solving difficult problems were found during their building. Here are some interesting facts and figures—there are many more you can find out about.

The world's longest bridge

The Akashi Kaikyo Bridge, in Japan, is the longest suspension bridge in the world. It stretches 12,828 feet (3,909 m)—that is about as long as eight skyscrapers laid end to end! The bridge was designed to be 12,825 feet (3,908 m) long, but an earthquake stretched the bridge another 3 feet (1 m)!

Brooklyn Bridge

When it was finished in 1883, the Brooklyn Bridge was the longest suspension bridge in the world. It would take four Brooklyn Bridges to span the same distance as the Akashi Kaikyo Bridge.

During building, the Brooklyn Bridge had many firsts. It was the first suspension bridge to use steel for its cables—all 14,283 miles (23,000 km) of them. It was the first to use explosives inside caissons (concrete tubes). The caisson walls were lined with sheets of iron to fireproof them. They were painted white to reflect the light and helped the builders to see. About 144,000 vehicles cross the bridge every day.

The skybridge between the Petronas Towers, in Malaysia, is the highest footbridge in the world.

You can find out about some of the challenges engineers meet when they design and build a bridge by using a construction set to build your own. Construction set parts can be screwed together and made into towers, decks, and even cable-stays.

Strength and stability are just as important in a construction set as they are in a life-sized structure. Many of today's engineers and architects started with construction sets. They are still building with them—the construction sets just grew bigger.

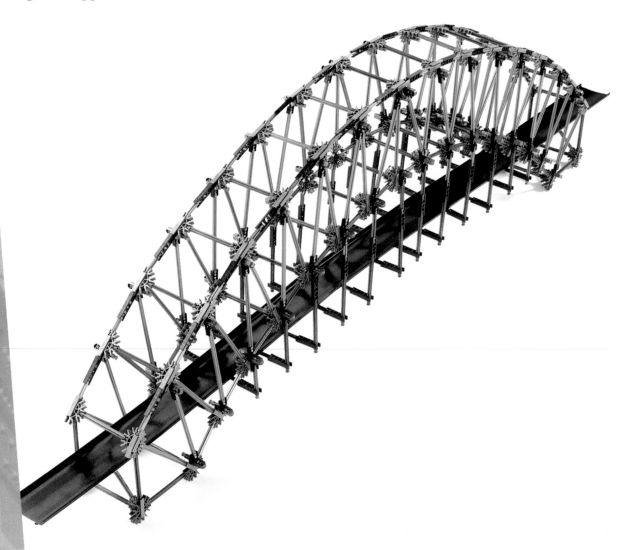

▲ Construction sets are a great way to learn about strong and stable bridges.

GLOSSARY

abutments	supports at the end of a bridge
anchored	attached to something heavy to stop moving
beam	a long piece of strong wood or metal that stretches across a gap and supports a structure above
brace	something fastened to an object to keep it stiff and straight, just like the braces worn on teeth
canals	waterways made by humans
cement	an ingredient in concrete which makes the concrete harden like stone
device	a machine or tool designed to do a particular job
embankments	mounds of earth made by humans to carry a road or railroad
engineers	people who design and build large structures
expansion	growing or getting bigger
fiberglass	a material made with threads of glass
flexible	able to bend without breaking
girders	long, thick beams that support part of a structure
hangers	pieces of metal that join the vertical steel cables to the horizontal cables on a suspension bridge
Kevlar	very strong human-made material
materials	anything used to make a structure
pile drivers	powerful machines that push large metal or concrete poles into the ground like a hammer
reinforced	made stronger
rivets	pins which are used to fasten sheets of metal together
spandrels	supports that connect an arch to the road deck that the arch holds up
stable	something that will not wobble or fall
structure	something that is made up of many parts joined together
suspension	supported from above
trusses	beams made up of different lengths of steel or wood
welding	joining pieces of metal together by heating their edges until they melt into one

INDEX